NORWAY

NORWAY
The Land of Mountains and Fjords

Chris McNab

This new edition first published in 2024

Reprinted in 2026

Copyright © 2020 Amber Books Ltd

All rights reserved. No part of this publication may be reproduced, stored in a retrieval system, or transmitted in any form or by any means, electronic, mechanical, photocopying, recording, or otherwise, without prior written permission of the copyright holder.

Published by
Amber Books Ltd
United House
North Road
London
N7 9DP
United Kingdom
www.amberbooks.co.uk
Instagram: amberbooksltd
Facebook: amberbooks
Twitter: @amberbooks
Pinterest: amberbooksltd

ISBN 978-1-83886-438-5

Project Editor: Anna Brownbridge, Sarah Uttridge
Design: Mark Batley
Picture Research: Terry Forshaw, Justin Willsdon

Printed in China

Contents

Introduction	6
Glaciers and Fjords	8
The Islands	50
Provinces and Towns	106
Oslo	152
Picture Credits	224

Introduction

In Norway, nature demands our full attention. There is the dramatic beauty of the glacier-carved fjords, crisscrossing to form islands scattered like jigsaw pieces over the sea. The steep Scandinavian Mountains are the country's rocky spine, giving birth to vast rivers of jagged ice. Ice and tundra cloak the far north archipelago of Svalbard, where most islands are inhabited only by fierce polar bears and their prey. During the long, dark winters here, the sky gives a sometimes nightly show, as the solar wind

brings charged particles to collide with our atmosphere. In the country's 47 National Parks, hikers across the wilderness will be lucky to meet anyone or anything other than a herd of reindeer, or perhaps a shy wolverine or lynx. Along the coasts, fishermen and women depend on the seasonal swims of cod and herring, just as they have for thousands of years. Even in the centre of Oslo, nature cannot be forgotten, as the waters of the Oslofjord still bring their daily catch, while the iconic Opera House looks ready to calve, glacier-like, into the harbour.

ABOVE:
Northern Lights, Nordland
The chances of seeing the aurora borealis are highest between October and March.

OPPOSITE:
Reine, Moskenesøya, Lofoten Archipelago
Traditional seasonal fishermen's cottages, called *rorbu*, jut over the water on stilts to give easy access to boats.

Glaciers & Fjords

Norway's landscape has been shaped by ice, which carved features such as fjords, vast plains and trough valleys. During the last ice age, nearly the whole country was covered by an ice sheet. Today, Norway has around 1600 glaciers, a number that may fall to a few dozen by 2100 if the global climate emergency is not addressed. Glaciers are bodies of densely packed ice that move slowly downhill under their own weight. As they flow, they deform and crack, creating crevasses and columns called seracs. Outside polar regions, glaciers build up at high altitudes, over many years or centuries, where snow falls faster than it melts. A large body of glacial ice that is not constrained by topographical features, lying evenly over the tops of mountains, is called an ice cap. Norway's largest ice caps are in the Svalbard Archipelago.

The word 'fjord' comes from the Norwegian for a narrow body of water. In scientific terms, a fjord is a long, narrow sea inlet, carved by a glacier. Over geological time, a glacier cuts a deep U-shaped valley as the rocks it carries rub away at the bedrock, while layers of ice called lenses freeze into the ground, wedging it apart. When the valley is flooded by the sea, it becomes a fjord. If the valley forms above sea level, a freshwater lake is created. Most fjords are deeper than the coastal sea into which they empty. They often have a shallower sill at their sea mouth, formed by the glacier's collected debris as well as the reduced erosion at the glacier's snout. There are around 1200 fjords in Norway, giving it a coastline of 29,000km (18,000 miles), the longest in Europe. The longest and deepest is Sognefjord, 205km (127 miles) long and up to 1308m (4291ft) deep.

OPPOSITE:
Folgefonna Glacier, Hordaland
In summer, guided hikes on the 168sq km (65sq mile) Folgefonna Glacier make a popular day trip. Up to 1662m (5452ft) above sea level on the Folgefonna Peninsula of western Norway, this plateau glacier is the third largest ice cap in mainland Norway, after Jostedal and Svartisen.

LEFT:
Juklavass Glacier, Hordaland
At the edge of Folgefonna National Park, Juklavass Glacier is a destination for skiing, blue ice hiking and, for the most adventurous, roped descents into vertiginous crevasses. Views from the glacier encompass the Rosendal Alps and, to the west, the North Sea.

ABOVE:
Negri Glacier, Spitsbergen, Svalbard Archipelago
This vast glacier, covering about 1180sq km (460sq miles), debouches into Storfjord, which separates the island of Spitsbergen from the smaller islands of Barentsøya and Edgeøya to the east. The 18 largest glaciers in Norway are in the Svalbard Archipelago.

OVERLEAF:
Kleivafossen, Briksdal Glacier, Sogn og Fjordane
Walkers to Briksdal Glacier must pass over the spray-drenched bridge by the Kleivafossen waterfall. Here the Briksdalselva drops 40m (130ft) over a step in the glacially carved valley below its source glacier. Briksdal Glacier is an arm of Jostedal, the largest ice cap in mainland Europe.

Briksdal Glacier, Sogn og Fjordane
A northern arm of the famous Jostedal, Briksdal terminates in a small glacial lake. The steep tongue (pictured) is prone to avalanches, making it dangerous to approach too close to the deeply churned ice. Global warming is making Briksdal recede, which may soon seasonally disconnect it from Jostedal.

Iceberg off Austfonna Glacier, Nordaustlandet, Svalbard Archipelago
Norway's largest glacier, and the third largest in Europe (after Severny Island in Russia and Vatnajökull in Iceland), Austfonna covers 7800sq km (3000sq miles). Its snout regularly calves into the Arctic Ocean due to its relatively great movement of 3.8km (2.4 miles) per year.

Nigard Glacier, Sogn og Fjordane
Avalanches, as well as sudden waves caused by calving on Nigardsbrevatn, are common, so hikes on Nigardsbreen must be taken with an experienced guide. The grey ice surface is caused by dust, while the blue tint is the result of dense ice absorbing other colours of light more easily than blue.

OPPOSITE:
Saltfjellet–Svartisen National Park, Nordland
With Svartisen Glacier as its centrepiece, this National Park encompasses deep fjords, mountain lakes, rugged peaks, high moorlands and forests. Many Sámi cultural monuments are also clustered here, including traces of ancient circular sacrificial sites.

ABOVE:
Trolltunga, Ringedalsvatnet, Hordaland
Jutting from the cliffside about 700m (2300ft) above the glacial lake Ringedalsvatnet is a slab of gneiss, named 'Troll's Tongue'. According to myth, trolls are cruel creatures that can be turned to stone by sunlight. In fact, the formation was created by glacial erosion, as ice froze in the crevices of the mountain and broke off large, irregular chunks.

Vatterfjord, Lofoten Islands, Nordland
While not technically a fjord, this narrow stretch of sea earns the name in the Norwegian sense as it winds its way through the bays and islets of Austvågøy, in the Lofoten Archipelago. Although north of the Arctic Circle, Lofoten has an anomalously mild climate due to the warmth of the Gulf Stream.

LEFT:
Lysefjord, Rogaland
On a clear day, the view eastward from the summit of Preikestolen stretches nearly as far as the isolated village of Lysebotn, at the head of the fjord. The village is reached only by boat and a road that makes 27 hairpin turns. Luckily, the road is open only when ice-free.

ABOVE:
Preikestolen, Lysefjord
'Pulpit Rock' is a spectacular granite cliff that, until the local tourist organization decided to promote it in the early 20th century, was known as Hyvlatonnå, meaning 'Planed Tooth'. The cliff rises above Lysefjord, which itself means 'Light Fjord' due to the pale granite of its rocks. Below Preikestolen, the fjord is over 400m (1300ft) deep, while at the sea end it reaches a depth of only 13m (43ft).

OPPOSITE AND ABOVE:
Undredal, Aurlandsfjord, Sogn og Fjordane
With a population of 600, including 500 goats, Undredal lies on Aurlandsfjord, a branch of Norway's longest fjord, the 205-km (127-mile) Sognefjord. There are few villages along Aurlandsfjord thanks to its steep cliffs. Until 1988 and the construction of two lengthy tunnels, Undredal was accessible only by boat.

LEFT:
Austdal Glacier, Sogn og Fjordane
Another of Jostedal's 50 arms, Austdal calves into Styggevatnet glacial lake. Kayakers here must often paddle their way between towering icebergs. At the opposite end of the lake is a hydroelectric dam and powerplant, making use of a 1180m (3870ft) drop to power its turbines.

Nordfjord, Sogn og Fjordan
This 106-km (66-mile) fjord is born in the east as runoff from Jostedal Glacier, while its mouth empties into the Norwegian Sea between the islands of Vågsøy and Bremangerlandet. Many of the settlements along the fjord have made their living from fishing since Viking times.

Olden, Nordfjord, Sogn og Fjordan
On the northern shore of Nordfjord, Olden is a popular hub for visits to the Briksdal Glacier, which lies at the opposite end of the long Oldedalen river valley. Until 1934, the wooden Old Olden Church, dating from 1759, was the only church in the valley.

LEFT:
Kjerag, Lysefjord, Rogaland
The 1110-m (3640-ft) Kjerag mountain lies towards the eastern end of Lysefjord. Its northern face is a sheer cliff, plunging 984m (3228ft) to the water below. It is a popular destination for hiking, climbing and BASE (building, antenna, span and earth) jumping, the last sport being by far the most statistically risky, even for world-renowned jumpers. The Kjeragfossen waterfall (pictured) is active for only five months of the year.

ABOVE:
Kjeragbolten, Lysefjord
The 'Kjerag Boulder' is a 5 cubic m (180 cubit ft) rock wedged between two faces of the Kjerag. The rock is a glacial deposit, stranded by the same ice sheet that carved the fjord below, around 50,000 years ago. For some visitors, it is the ultimate dare to walk onto Kjeragbolten itself, undeterred by the fact that there is an immediate 241-m (791-ft) drop below, followed by a steep slope another 735m (2411ft) down to the fjord.

ABOVE:
Geiranger, Geirangerfjord, Møre og Romsdal
Geiranger, with a permanent population of just 250, is one of Norway's busiest cruise ship ports. The 2015 film *The Wave* imagined the outcome of a not-inconceivable disaster: that a rockfall from the nearby Åkerneset crevasse, which is currently widening, would cause an 80-m (260-ft) tsunami, destroying the town. A vertiginously sited and now deserted farm beneath the crevasse was probably the model for the farm in Henrik Ibsen's 1865 play *Brand*.

OPPOSITE:
Aurlandsfjord, Sogn og Fjordane
This 962-m (3156-ft) deep, narrow fjord stretches for 29km (18 miles). Much of it is included in UNESCO's West Norwegian Fjords World Heritage Site. The nearby village of Flåm boasts the only train station in this county, where transport for the scattered population is hampered by soaring mountains and endlessly branching fjords.

Nærøyfjord, Sogn og Fjordane
The village of Gudvangen possesses a breathtaking view down the UNESCO-listed Nærøyfjord. At its narrowest point, the fjord is 250m (820ft) wide, while the surrounding peaks are up to 1700m (5580ft) high.

Ulvikafjord, Hordaland
This northern branch of Hardangerfjord extends for about 8km (5 miles), reaching its end near Ulvik. In 1940, the village was burned by German soldiers in retaliation for harbouring Norwegian resistance fighters. Today, the settlement is a centre for hiking, waterskiing and cider-tasting.

OPPOSITE:
Bearded Seal, Lilliehookfjord, Spitsbergen, Svalbard Archipelago
The Lilliehook Glacier calves into this branch of the Krossfjord, providing resting places for bearded seals. Found in and around the Arctic Ocean, the bearded seal reaches 2.7m (8.8ft) long. It is known for its complex and geographically variable 'singing', consisting of trills, moans and sweeps.

TOP RIGHT:
Arctic Fox, Spitsbergen
In summer, the Arctic fox's thick fur turns brown-grey (pictured), while in winter it is pure white for camouflage against the frozen tundra. With foot pads covered in fur and a low surface-area-to-volume ratio, this fox starts to shiver only when the temperature drops to −70°C (−94°F).

BOTTOM RIGHT:
Reindeer, Troms
Both male and female reindeer grow antlers every year in spring and summer, but only males use them to fight with other males, during the autumn mating season. Males lock antlers, trying to push the other away. The winning males can gain as many as 20 mates.

Orca, Troms
The Norwegian coast, particularly during the winter months, is one of the best places in the world to watch orcas, also known as killer whales. Resident orcas, up to 8m (26ft) long, travel through the northern fjord system on the hunt for herring. Orca pods often surround herring trawlers, trying to share the catch.

OPPOSITE:

Atlantic Puffin, Runde, Møre og Romsdal

The island of Runde is home to around 100,000 Atlantic puffins, as well as black-legged kittiwakes, common guillemots, razorbills and many other seabirds. The Atlantic puffin dives for small fish in the cool waters of the northern Atlantic Ocean. It spends most of its life at sea, resting on the water surface. It returns to its coastal colony only to breed in spring.

ABOVE:

Eurasian Oystercatcher, Runde

This migratory wader breeds in northern Europe and Asia, spending its winters farther south. It often uses its strong red beak for prising open the shells of oysters and mussels, picking its moment at low tide. Sometimes, the bivalve is quick enough to slam shut its shell, trapping the bird's beak and resulting in catastrophe as the tide rises.

ABOVE:
Rock Ptarmigan, Troms
With its winter plumage camouflaging it against the snow, and feathered legs for warmth, the rock ptarmigan is resident year round on Norway's rocky mountainsides and tundra. In spring, its feathers moult from white to brown.

RIGHT
White-Tailed Eagle, Nordland
A resident in western Norway, this sea eagle snatches fish from near the water surface, usually wetting only its feet. It will also prey on smaller birds and mammals, snatch food from otters, and even resort to carrion in winter.

OPPOSITE:
Hardangervidda, Buskerud, Hordaland and Telemark
Covering approximately 6500sq km (2500sq miles), Hardangervidda is the largest peneplain, or eroded plain, in Europe, formed by the action of ice age glaciers. With an average height of 1100m (3500ft), the plateau has a year-round alpine climate in which lichen, sphagnum mosses and coarse grasses are able to thrive.

BELOW:
Jotunheimen, Sogn og Fjordane and Oppland
This region, part of the Scandinavian Mountains, is home to Norway's highest peaks, including the tallest of all, 2469-m (8100-ft) Galdhøpiggen. Mostly above the treeline, the Jotunheimen flora is largely low-growing, lime-loving flowerless plants, but Norway's highest growing flowering plant, the glacier crowfoot, can also be found here.

The Islands

Around 55,000 islands lie off Norway's intricate coastline, the majority no more than rocky stacks home to nesting seabirds or resting seals. Many of the islands are skerries, formed at the outlets of fjords where these flooded glacial valleys grew at right angles to the coast and met with cross-valleys, forming a complex network of ice-scoured channels and island blocks. Close to the far northern coast of Finnmark is the misty tundra of Magerøya, where the midnight sun hovers over the sea. To the southwest are the icily beautiful Vesterålen and Lofoten Archipelagos, where fishermen have caught Arctic cod for millennia. In the far south are the neat cottage islands of the Oslofjord. In between are numerous lesser-known islands, each with their own draw, from pretty Hidra to mountainous Sandhornøya.

The Kingdom of Norway also has two remote jurisdictions, the volcanic island of Jan Mayen and the Svalbard Archipelago. Jan Mayen, around 600km (370 miles) northeast of Iceland in the Arctic Ocean, is a military base and scientific station, rarely visited by ordinary travellers. The Svalbard Archipelago, which lies midway between continental Norway and the North Pole, draws cruise ships and intrepid travellers with its fragile glaciers, polar bears and the unique frontier settlement of Longyearbyen. The archipelago, administered by a governor appointed by the Norwegian government, is covered by the 1920 Svalbard Treaty, which gives equal rights to mine and carry out commercial activities to its 46 signatories. However, only Russia and Norway make use of these rights. Six National Parks protect the archipelago's precious environment.

OPPOSITE:
Isfjord, Spitsbergen, Svalbard Archipelago
The largest island in the Svalbard Archipelago, Spitsbergen is also the largest of all Norway's islands. As the only permanently inhabited island in Svalbard, Spitsbergen makes its living from mining, research and tourism. Despite its dramatic re-imagining in the British TV series *Fortitude* (2015–18), Spitsbergen is almost crime-free.

LEFT:
Andøya, Vesterålen Archipelago, Nordland
The population of this Arctic island, the most northerly in the Vesterålen Archipelago, relies on cod fishing, peat production and cloudberries. These tart, amber-coloured fruits, regarded as a delicacy in Scandinavia, grow in boggy tundra, where other crops are difficult. The berries can be mixed with whipped cream and sugar to make *multekrem* (cloudberry cream) dessert or stirred into yoghurt and ice cream.

ABOVE:
Askøy, Hordaland
Since 1992, when the Askøy suspension bridge linked the island of Askøy with the city of Bergen, just across the Byfjord, the population has grown rapidly. However, the northern and western regions of the island are still sparsely populated, home to isolated fishing hamlets and strawberry farms. The island gets its name from the Ask ('ash tree') *Kongsgård*, or royal estate, sited here because of the temperate climate.

Sildpollneset Peninsula, Austvågøya, Lofoten Archipelago, Nordland
One of Lofoten's five main islands, Austvågøya has the rugged archipelago's highest peak: 1146-m (3760-ft) Higravtinden. Local artist Gunnar Berg (1863–93) drew international attention to the island with his Romantic paintings of its seascapes and fishermen, before his death at the age of 30.

ABOVE:
Skagsanden Beach, Flagstadøya, Lofoten Archipelago
On Skagsanden beach, a seasonal fisherman's hut gives easy access to the sea. Facing northward and with a wide, open horizon, Skagsanden is an ideal spot to watch the northern lights during winter. In summer, the golden sand forms intricate patterns as a stream ripples into the sea.

OPPOSITE:
Mail Boxes, Moskenesøya, Lofoten Archipelago
The Lofoten postman drives 200km (125 miles) each day to deliver post and newspapers around the archipelago. During winter, visits from the postman can be a vital link to the outside world for older residents. Although the main, cross-archipelago road, the E10, is continuously ploughed, side-roads can remain impassable for some time. Tractor-owning locals do their best to keep their communities moving.

RIGHT TOP:
View from Averøya, Møre og Romsdal
The dramatic 8-km (5-mile) Atlantic Ocean Road connects Averøya, along with other islands and skerries in its archipelago, with the mainland, via a series of causeways, viaducts and bridges. The route, completed in 1989, is regularly named as one of the world's best road trips.

RIGHT BOTTOM:
Barentsøya, Svalbard Archipelago
Barentsøya is heavily glaciated, with its tundra home only to hardy fauna such as reindeer, polar bears, kittiwakes and Arctic foxes. The island was named after the Dutch explorer William Barents (c.1550–97), who probably discovered nearby Spitsbergen but never actually sighted his namesake.

OPPOSITE:
Gimsøy Church, Gimsøya, Lofoten Archipelago
This traditional wooden 'long church', built in 1876, consists of a single long nave for the congregation, with a smaller and narrower choir and vestibule attached. The bell tower rests on the vestibule. The church has seating for 300, yet the island's population is currently around 180.

Stokmarknes, Hadseløya, Vesterålen Archipelago
The largest town on the island of Hadseløya, Stokmarknes hosts the Coastal Express shipping museum and the 1956 steamer MS *Finnmarken* (painted in black and red). A more modern ship with the same name, owned by the same company, still cruises the Norwegian coast and islands.

Holdøya, Lofoten Archipelago
From the north coast of Austvågøya, the view takes in the islet of Holdøya, linked to the larger island by a causeway. In the background, across the Hadselfjord, are the mountains of Hadseløya in Vesterålen, rising to 657m (2156ft).

Sommarøy Bridge, Kvaløya–Sommarøya, Troms
The island of Kvaløya is linked with the smaller and less populous island of Sommarøya by the single-lane Sommarøy Bridge. Traffic lights, said to malfunction in windy weather, prevent head-on collisions. In summer, the white beaches of Sommarøya are popular with trippers from the city of Tromsø.

Lindøya, Oslo
Lying in the Oslofjord, just south of Oslo, the island of Lindøya is a favoured location for Oslovians' summer cabins. The extraordinary Expressionist composition *The Scream*, by Oslo resident Edvard Munch (1863–1944), was inspired by a sunset walk beside the Oslofjord in 1892.

ABOVE:
Nyksund, Langøya, Vesterålen Archipelago
Although the site of Nyksund was populated for centuries, the village became a ghost town in the 1970s due to its lack of infrastructure. Thanks to a restoration project, the village is now home to a handful of hardy residents year round.

RIGHT:
Petter Dass Chapel, Husøya, Nordland
Opened in 1997, this chapel commemorates the Lutheran priest and poet Petter Dass (c.1647–1707). He wrote many Norwegian hymns that are still sung today, including 'Herre Gud, Ditt Dyre Navn og Aere' ('Good Lord, Thy Precious Name and Glory').

Trollholmen, Magerøya
The islet of Trollholmen lies in Skipsfjord, on the eastern side of Magerøya. The islet and its fishing hamlet are accessed by bridge and boat. Not far away, archaeologists have found evidence of human habitation dating back 10,000 years.

PREVIOUS PAGE AND RIGHT:
Bråsvell Glacier, Nordaustlandet, Svalbard Archipelago
This 'ice wall' is an outlet of the vast Austfonna ice cap, which is around 200km (125 miles) in circumference. Bråsvell glacier tongue extends 10km (6 miles) into the Arctic Ocean on the southern coast of Nordaustlandet, the second largest island in the Svalbard Archipelago. Entirely uninhabited, three-quarters of Nordaustlandet is covered by ice, while the remaining tundra is the haunt of cold-tolerating creatures such as reindeer, walruses and ivory gulls.

OVERLEAF:
Prins Karls Forland, Svalbard Archipelago
The entirety of the uninhabited Prins Karls Forland is protected as the Forlandet National Park, where the world's most northerly colony of common guillemots can be found. The island was named in around 1612 by English whalers, after their Prince Charles, who was later to become the ill-fated King Charles I of England, Scotland and Ireland.

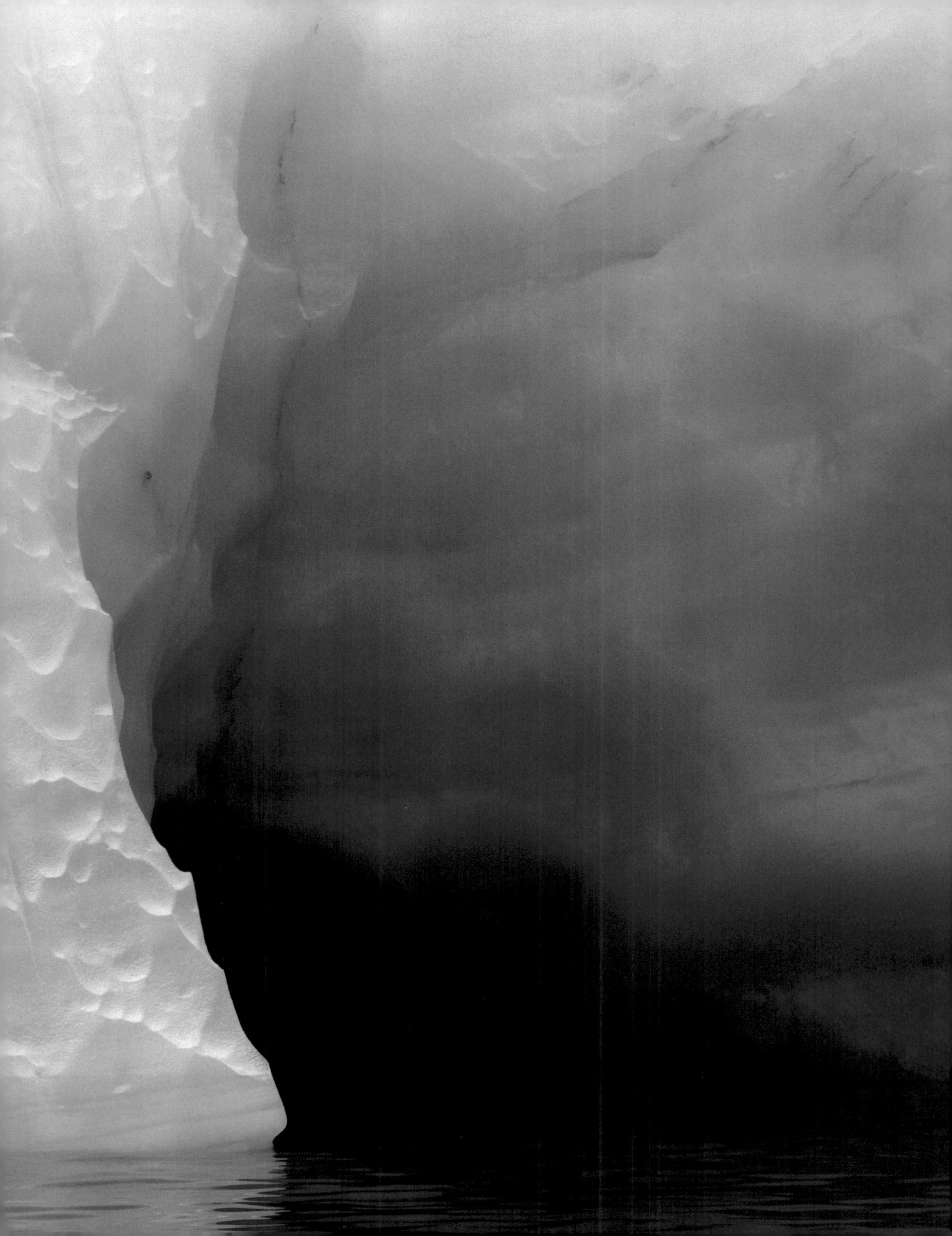

ABOVE:
Vågsøy, Sogn og Fjordane
Vågsøy is connected to the mainland by the 1224-m (4016-ft) cantilever Måløy Bridge. The bridge was built to withstand winds of up to 270km/h (170mph), but cars driving across cannot do the same, so it is closed during storms. Due to the island's perilously rocky coastline, it has four lighthouses.

OPPOSITE:
Kannesteinen, Vågsøy
Around 3m (10ft) tall, this mushroom rock has been shaped by the continuous pounding of ocean waves and pebbles against its 'stem', while its 'cap' remains above the tide. The rock is formed mostly of the globally rare, although locally common, metamorphic rock eclogite. It contains stripes or lumps of red garnet and green omphacite.

LEFT:
Ringvassøya, Troms
This Arctic Circle island, with an area of 663sq km (256sq miles), has a permanent population of just 1300. The economy here is heavily dependent on dried and salted cod, although tourism has also played a role in recent decades. Since 1988, the island has been linked with the mainland, via the neighbouring island of Kvaløya, by a 1650-m (5410-ft) undersea tunnel. Norway currently has more than 30 undersea tunnels.

ABOVE:
Sakrisøya and Moskenesøya, Lofoten Archipelago
The islet of Sakrisøya lies off the coast of Moskenesøya, linked by the European route E10 highway. This winding, never-forgotten road begins on Moskenesøya near the village of Å (with its frequently stolen road sign) and ends in the city of Luleå, in Sweden. Tiny Sakrisøya offers cosy guesthouses and restaurants, plus views across Reinefjord to the 675-m (2215-ft) conical Mount Olstind.

Sørøya, Finnmark
In 1945, Sørøya saw heavy fighting between the Norwegian Resistance and German troops. In February of that year, more than 500 civilians (of around 1000 in total) were evacuated to Scotland in Operation Open Door. Today, the island is home to many Sámi people, some of whom practise a traditional reindeer-herding lifestyle.

Bergsfjord, Senja, Troms
This vast island, around 1586 sq km (613 sq miles), is often called 'Norway in miniature' because of its diverse scenery. The wild western coast is mountainous and carved by fjords, while the milder eastern portion is lower and carpeted by forests and farms. The 1147-m (3763-ft) Gisund Bridge links it to the mainland.

Sula, Møre og Romsdal
Most of the population of Sula lives along the northern and eastern shores, while the craggy, heather-covered southwestern portion and the many surrounding islets are home mainly to nesting seabirds. However, Sula is known for its jazz and folk scene and was the birthplace of jazz trumpeter Nils Petter Molvær and the Brazz Brothers.

LEFT AND ABOVE:
Longyearbyen, Spitsbergen, Svalbard Archipelago
With a permanent population of around 2100, Longyearbyen is the world's most northerly town, as all settlements farther north are purely scientific outposts. Since the mining industry dominates here, around 60 per cent of residents are male. Hardly any residents are aged over 65, because everyone living here must be able to support themselves with their own funds if they do not have an employment contract. In fact, those without a job or other income are deported to the mainland.

Longyearbyen, Spitsbergen
Named after American mining magnate John Munro Longyear, Longyearbyen was founded in 1906. Clustered in neat rows, homes here are usually owned by mining companies or the government. To ease monotony and help with identification, facades are painted in bright colours, with rules governing which colours can be used where.

LEFT:

Miner's Apartment, Pyramiden
Between 1910 and 1998, Pyramiden was a bustling place, with a primary school, restaurant, hotel, theatre, library, art studio and sports centre. Today, the apartments and many public areas look as if they were abandoned in a hurry. To encourage tourism to the ghost town and surrounding tundra, the Arktikugol mining company has reopened the hotel.

ABOVE:

Lenin Statue, Pyramiden, Spitsbergen
The most northerly statue of Vladimir Lenin stands in the central square of the abandoned Russian coal-mining settlement of Pyramiden. After the last coal was extracted from the mine on 31 March 1998, all of the 1000 residents swiftly left. The nearest town is Longyearbyen, around 50km (30 miles) away.

Svalbard Reindeer
The smallest subspecies of reindeer, *Rangifer tarandus platyrhynchus* is endemic to the Svalbard Archipelago, where it lives on most unglaciated land. The subspecies has relatively short legs and long, thick fur, which makes it appear yet shorter-legged than it is. Males weigh 65–90kg (140–200lb), while male North American woodland caribou, the largest subspecies, weigh 110–210kg (240–460lb).

Polar Bear, Svalbard Archipelago
In winter, polar bears can be met anywhere in the Svalbard Archipelago, which is why it is illegal to leave the town of Longyearbyen without a gun or another means of warding off these fearsome predators. In summer, the bears follow the shrinking sea ice northward so they can hunt for their favourite prey, seals, as they surface at ice holes.

LEFT:
Stockfish Rack, Svolvær, Austvågøya, Lofoten Archipelago
Pyramidal stockfish racks, called *hjell*, are a common sight in Lofoten, as well as on foreshores across the country, from February to May. Stockfish is not salted, but dried by cold air and wind. During the process, cold-adapted bacteria ferments the fish, preserving it for several years.

ABOVE TOP:
Fishing Boats
Norway is the world's second largest exporter of fish by value, after China. Fish comes only after oil and natural gas in Norway's list of exports. On the islands, fishing of cod, herring, halibut and other cold-water species has been the foremost industry for millennia. Small-scale coastal vessels still make up a large proportion of the national fishing fleet.

ABOVE BOTTOM:
Catch on the Quay, Runde, Møre og Romsdal
Before being hung to dry, fish must be bled, gutted, decapitated and washed in seawater. After its time on the *hjell*, stockfish is stored indoors, in a cool and dry loft. During the process, the fish loses around 80 per cent of its water. Stockfish is used in traditional recipes such as *lutefisk*, which is made with lye.

ABOVE:
Fishing Nets, Lofoten Archipelago
Fish stocks in the waters around the Lofoten Islands are seasonal, with the Arctic cod season, known as the Lofotfiske, coming in February to April, when the fish arrive to spawn. In summer, local fishermen often sail to the waters off Finnmark to catch haddock.

RIGHT:
Herring Boat off Kvaløya, Troms
Herring is vital to the Troms fishing industry. In winter, the fish swim deep into the fjord system looking for the perfect place to spawn in spring. As well as having immense commercial value, herring are a vital link in the food chain for orcas, dolphins, whales, cod, tuna, salmon and many seabirds.

Vippefyr, Verdens Ende, Tjøme, Vestfold
This replica of a *vippefyr*, or tipping lantern, stands at 'World's End' on the southernmost promontory of the island of Tjøme. During the 17th and 18th centuries, these lanterns were sometimes erected as lighthouses along the coasts of Scandinavia. Wood or coal was burned in the basket, which could be raised or lowered using the lever.

BELOW AND RIGHT:

Global Seed Vault, Spitsbergen
Opened in 2008, the seed vault provides secure back-up storage for seeds held in 1700 gene banks worldwide, in case of global or regional disasters. The bank is paid for by the Norwegian government and various charitable organizations. Spitsbergen was chosen as a location because of its permafrost, which aids preservation in combination with refrigeration units, and lack of tectonic activity. In case of the melting of ice caps, the bank is also built 130m (430ft) above sea level. The vault has the capacity to hold 4.5 million batches of seeds (or 2.5 billion individual seeds), which is twice the number of existing crop varieties. Currently, the vault keeps around 968,000 batches from across the globe. The facade features an illuminated artwork by Norwegian artist Dyveke Sanne.

OVERLEAF:

Northern Lights, EISCAT Svalbard Radar, Spitsbergen
The European Incoherent Scatter Scientific Association radar system monitors interaction between the Sun and Earth, which creates disturbances in the ionosphere and magnetosphere. The aurora borealis, or northern lights, are the result of disturbances caused by the solar wind, when these electrically charged particles collide with gaseous particles in the Earth's atmosphere. Around the poles, the Earth's magnetic field is weaker than elsewhere, so it is unable to deflect the charged particles.

Provinces and Towns

The mainland is dominated by the Scandinavian Mountains, a steep, rugged chain arcing for 1700km (1100 miles) from the southwest to the border with Finland. Thanks to these mountains, Norway's average elevation is 460m (1510ft) and nearly a third of its land is alpine tundra. Galdhøpiggen, in Oppland, is Norway's highest peak, at 2469m (8100ft). The mountains split the landscape into physical and ecological regions. To the west, the peaks, sliced by deep fjords, drop precipitously into the North and Norwegian Seas. The south coast and southeast lie lower, with pine- and spruce-covered hills between valleys patched with farms. Through Northern Norway, moving into the Arctic Circle and the counties of Nordland, Troms and Finnmark, the land slowly flattens, culminating in the vast Finnmarksvidda plateau.

The majority of Norway's 5.3 million inhabitants live in the southeast, in and around Oslo, and along the southern and southwestern coasts. The mountainous interior and the north remain sparsely populated. The only city with a population over 1 million is Oslo, followed in size by the coastal, university cities Bergen, Stavanger and Trondheim. The largest city in Northern Norway is Tromsø, with a population of just 75,000 yet far more vibrant than most would expect from its Arctic Circle location. Norway's cities and towns are not just bases from which to explore the mountains and waterfall-laced valleys, but jewels in their own right, with architecture ranging from perfectly preserved wooden cottages to Art Nouveau

OPPOSITE:
Ålesund, Møre og Romsdal
After a fire destroyed 800 of Ålesund's timber houses in 1904, the city centre was rebuilt in an unusually consistent Art Nouveau style. The city stretches across a small archipelago, with the brightly painted harbourfront buildings facing the waterway between central islands Nørvøya and Aspøya.

PREVIOUS PAGES:
Ålesund
With a backdrop of the Sunnmøre Alps and its glittering islands scattered in the Norwegian Sea, Ålesund is often described as the most beautiful city in Norway. As Norway's largest fishing port, it is also a busy and practical city. Legend has it that a settlement was founded here by Rollo (c.860–c.930), the same Viking who became the first Norse ruler of Normandy. A statue of him stands in a central park, a gift from the French city of Rouen.

BELOW AND RIGHT:
Hanseatic Museum, Bergen, Hordaland
This museum shows how merchants of the Hanseatic League lived and worked when, from 1360 to 1754, they traded stockfish and grain from these offices, lodgings and assembly halls. The Hanseatic League was a federation of merchant guilds and towns in northwestern Europe, growing from a handful of north German towns in the late 12th century. The museum is on two sites, including the Finnegården building on Bryggen, which was built in 1704.

Troldhaugen, Bergen
Troldhaugen ('Troll Hill') was the home of composer Edvard Grieg (1843–1907) and his wife, the soprano Nina Grieg, from 1885 until Edvard's death. Built for the Griegs by his cousin, the architect Schak Bull, the house presents typical living rooms of a wealthy late 19th-century family. Troldhaugen was named at Nina's suggestion, evoking the trolls in one of Grieg's most famous works, the incidental music for Henrik Ibsen's *Peer Gynt*. In the section known as 'In the Hall of the Mountain King' angry trolls can be heard taunting the protagonist.

LEFT:
Bergen Station
This imposing building was designed in 1913 by Jens Zetlitz Monrad Kielland in National Romantic style, a Nordic form of Art Nouveau. Influenced by heavy medieval and vernacular architecture, the style also reflected the lighter ideals of Art Nouveau. This can be seen in the main hall, where stone walls are offset by the elegant roof.

ABOVE:
Sailors' Monument, Bergen
In Bergen's main square, Torgallmenningen, is this 7-m (23-ft) high monument to Norwegian sailors from Viking times to its erection in 1950. The work was sculpted by Dyre Vaa (1903–80), who often depicted Norwegian fairy tales and cultural figures. This vast square was originally created as a fire break.

OVERLEAF:
Flåm Station, Sogn og Fjordane
This station is the starting point for the 20-km (12-mile) Flåm Line. With a gradient of 5.5 per cent (1 in 18) at its steepest, this spectacular line runs from the inner end of Aurlandsfjord to Myrdal, where it connects with the Bergen Line. Along the way, the train runs through the pretty valley of Flåmsdalen.

OPPOSITE:

Stegastein Viewpoint, Sogn og Fjordane

Overlooking Aurlandsfjord, this viewpoint juts 30m (98ft) outward from the mountain wall and 650m (2132ft) up from the valley floor. The platform is constructed of steel and laminated pine. The busy road to the viewpoint from Aurland, often single-lane and switchbacking up the sheer mountainside, is more than enough adrenaline for some.

ABOVE:

Muskoxen, Dovrefjell–Sunndalsfjella National Park, Trøndelag

This National Park is one of the few places outside Arctic North America where muskoxen can be seen in the wild. The last known European muskox population died out in Sweden 9000 years ago. This population was introduced in 1947. The species, which should not be approached, is named after the strong odour given off by males during the seasonal rut.

Bryggen, Bergen
Bryggen ('The Dock') was the centre of Bergen's Hanseatic League activities from the 14th to the 18th centuries, when this was Norway's largest trading port. Bergen's wooden buildings have been destroyed by fire many times. Around a quarter of the Bryggen's structures date from immediately after the fire of 1702 but most are later, although a few stone cellars have lasted since the 15th century. Bryggen is a UNESCO World Cultural Heritage Site.

ALL PHOTOGRAPHS:
Fredrikstad, Østfold
Fredrikstad's Gamlebyen (Old Town) is one of the best-preserved fortified towns in northern Europe. Work on the town was begun in 1567 on the orders of Frederick II of Denmark, who wanted to rebuild the nearby city of Sarpsborg after it was burnt by Swedish invaders during the Northern Seven Years' War. The new town was given a wide water-filled moat, a drawbridge, high earth ramparts and a perimeter wall defended by cannons. Today, the cobbled streets of Gamlebyen, still defended by a star-shaped moat, are lined with 18th-century wooden and brick buildings. The oldest building of all is a stone storehouse dating back to 1674–91.

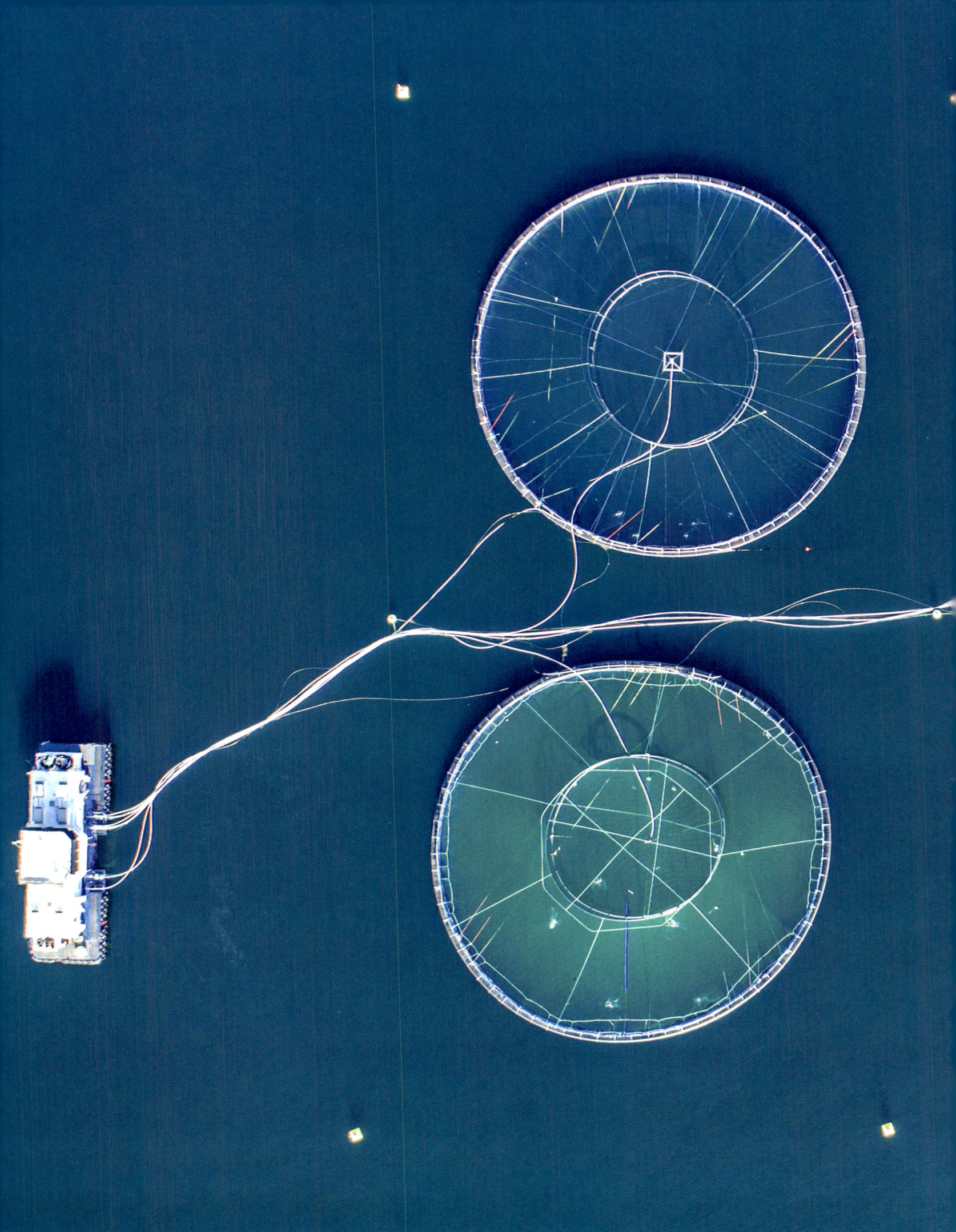

Salmon Farm, Hordaland
Hordaland is Norway's leading county for aquaculture, annually producing more than 100,000 tons of salmon and 20,000 tons of trout in more than 150 fish farms dotted through the fjords and rivers. Fish are usually kept in netted cages, preferably in water with a strong flow. Aquaculture here is carefully controlled to ensure that the balance of wild fish in the waterways is not disturbed.

Kilden Theatre, Kristiansand, Vest-Agder
This immense 2012 theatre and concert hall echoes the waters of the Skagerrak with its graceful oak waves. The oak was locally grown, a homage to the port's role as the country's largest exporter of oak from the 16th century.

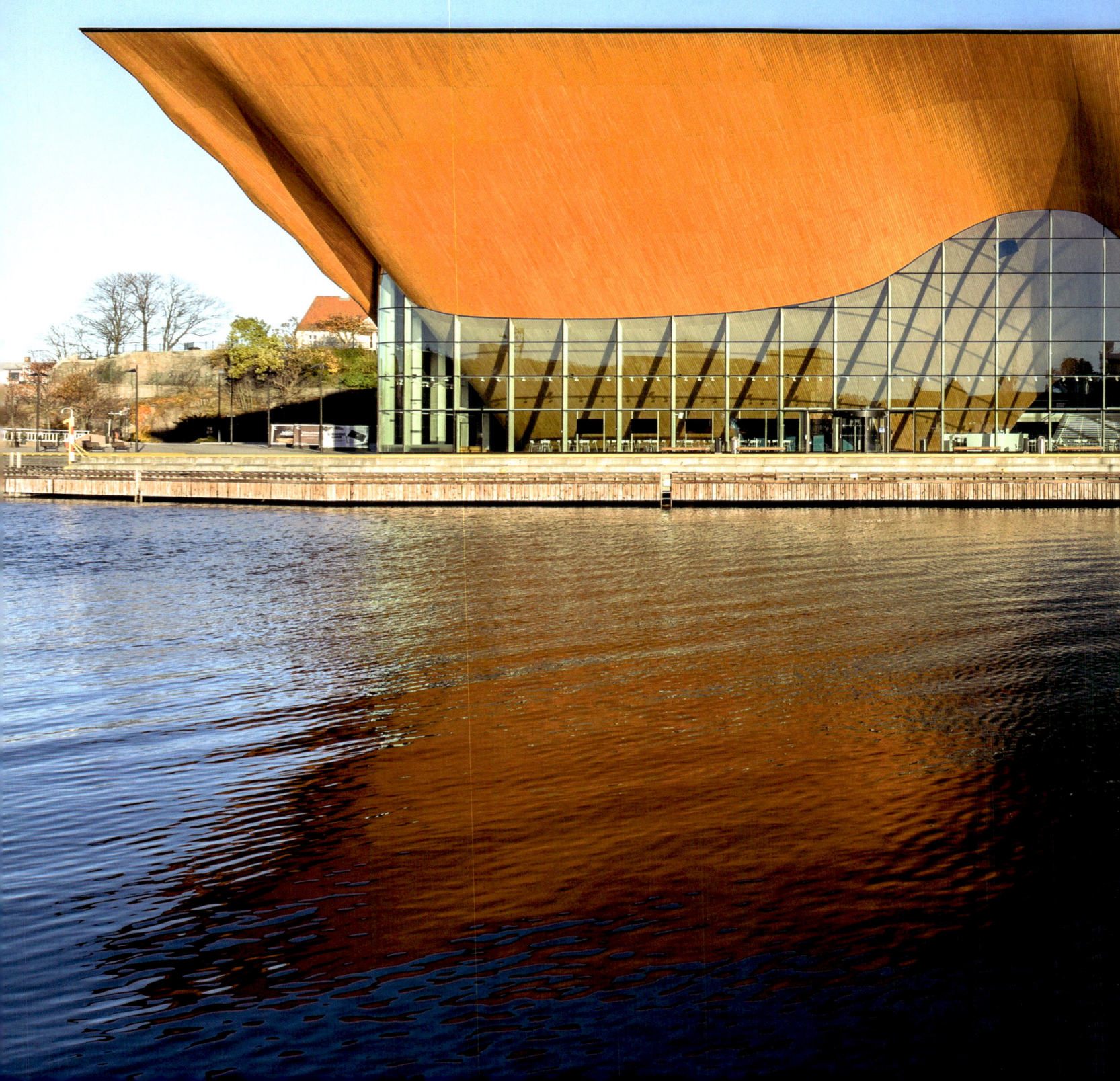

LEFT:
Odda, Hordaland
At the southern end of Sørfjord, the town of Odda is tucked between the fjord, towering mountains and Sandvinvatnet lake. A koiné language developed in the town during the 20th century, an entirely unique mix of the Norwegian dialects spoken by workers at the area's smelters.

ABOVE:
Heddal Stave Church, Telemark
The largest of Norway's 28 remaining stave churches was constructed in the early 13th century. Stave churches are timber framed, with a post (*stafr*) and lintel construction. Heddal is triple naved, with internal posts supporting three tiers of roof.

Mefjord, Senja, Troms
Inside the Arctic Circle, the fishing hamlets on Mefjord make their living largely from halibut and cod. In January and February, orcas and humpback whales are frequently seen in Mefjord, as they feed on the seasonal influx of herring. They are sometimes joined by much rarer fin whales, which reach 25.9m (85ft) long, making them second in size only to blue whales.

Near Tromsø, Troms
Sápmi, stretching across northern Norway, Sweden, Finland and the Murmansk Oblast of Russia, is the region traditionally inhabited by Sámi people. Today, around 10 per cent of Sámi are still connected to semi-nomadic reindeer herding. Concerns shared by many Sámi include climate change, land and resource rights, and cultural exploitation.

Midnight Sun, Tromsø, Troms
The island city of Tromsø lies in the Tromsøysundet strait, which is crossed by the 1036-m (3399-ft) Tromsø Bridge. With a population of 75,000, this is the third largest city north of the Arctic Circle, after Murmansk and Norilsk in Russia. Tromsø experiences the midnight sun between 18 May and 26 July.

LEFT:
Fish Market, Bergen
Bergen's outdoor fish market has been in operation since the 13th century. Its indoor extension has been open since 2012. The market was originally on Bryggen, but was moved to the inner stretch of Vågen bay in 1541 to prevent Hanseatic merchants gaining control over it.

BELOW:
Pancake Stall, Bergen
Named as a UNESCO City of Gastronomy, Bergen is most famous for its high-quality sustainable seafood, but is also gaining a reputation for street and international food. The city is one of the best places to try Norwegian specialities from *røkt laks* (smoked salmon) and *kjøttboller* (meatballs) to *krumkake* (rolls of waffle-like pancake, first cooked on an iron griddle then filled with whipped cream or any other sweet filling).

Nidaros Cathedral, Trondheim, Trøndelag
This Romanesque and Gothic cathedral was begun in 1070, over the burial site of King Olaf II of Norway. The king was canonized here by Bishop Grimketel, a year after his death in the Battle of Stiklestad in 1030. Both Olaf and Grimketel, an English missionary, were key to the Christianization of Norway. Olaf was baptized in Rouen in around 1014, while staying with Duke Richard II of Normandy.

ABOVE:

Husedalen Valley, Hordaland
The Husedalen Valley lies in Norway's largest National Park, Hardangervidda. From the Hardangervidda plateau, the Kinso River drops 1100m (3600ft), crashing over four spectacular waterfalls as it flows through the Husedalen Valley, before feeding into Hardangerfjord. The Hardangervidda plateau is above the treeline. Its alpine climate makes it the southern boundary for several Arctic plants and animals, including the Arctic fox and snowy owl. Its 8000-strong wild reindeer herds are among the largest in the world. The reindeer migrate from east to west across the plateau in spring, from their feeding to breeding grounds.

OPPOSITE:

Trollveggen, Møre og Romsdal
About 1100m (3600ft) tall from its base to its highest point, Trollveggen ('Troll Wall') is the tallest vertical rock face in Europe. In places, the summit ridge actually overhangs the base by 50m (160ft). Part of the Trolltindene ('Troll Peaks') massif, Trollveggen gets its name from folk tales about vicious trolls that were turned to stone by sunlight, or as punishment for their cruelty. The gneiss cliff is located in Reinheimen National Park, which preserves an alpine ecosystem where wolverines hunt herds of reindeer. The reindeer here are descended from semi-domesticated animals, so are less shy than most wild reindeer.

Tvindefossen Waterfall, Voss, Hordaland
Around 110m (360ft) high, this lacelike waterfall was painted by the great Norwegian Romantic artist Johan Christian Dahl (1788–1857), known for his monumental landscapes. In the late 1990s, the waterfall was receiving up to 272,000 visitors per year, thanks to a joke by a local guide. To fill a dull moment, he said the waters gave the gift of eternal youth – and the story spread.

LEFT:
Polaria, Tromsø
The world's northernmost aquarium, Polaria focuses on Arctic Ocean life. The central pool is home to bearded seals, the largest northern true seals, which reach 2.7m (8.9ft). The striking building, constructed in 1998, resembles ice floes that have been corrugated by Arctic waves.

ABOVE:
Ski Touring, Nordland
Den Norske Turistforening (Norwegian Trekking Association; DNT) branch-marks 7000km (4350 miles) of ski tracks. DNT also maintains 22,000km (13,600 miles) of marked foot trails. Members and non-members can stay at 550 cabins, some staffed and others self-service or no-service.

BELOW:
Rock Carvings, Alta
More than 6000 rock carvings have been found around Alta, forming Norway's only prehistoric World Heritage Site. Dated to between 4200 BC and 500 BC, the carvings depict herds of reindeer, some of them pregnant (pictured), behind fences or being hunted with spears and bows and arrows. Other carvings show scenes from daily life, including preparing food and fishing from boats, as well as shamanistic rituals involving bear worship and possible fertility rites. The carvings were made with rock chisels. Today, they have been cleaned and some are retouched with red paint by researchers.

RIGHT:
Alta Canyon, Finnmark
Known as Sautso in Northern Sámi, this canyon is 12km (7.5 miles) long and up to 420m (1380ft) deep, making it the largest in northern Europe. It was carved by the Altaelva River, on its way from the 22,000sq km (8500 sq mile) Finnmarksvidda plateau to the sea.

Rondane National Park, Hedmark and Oppland
Norway's oldest National Park, established in 1962, contains ten mountains over 2000m (6560ft). Nearly the entire park is above the treeline, its nutrient-poor soil and rocks covered by heather and lichen. The climate is arid, so persistent glaciers do not form. Roaming the park are wild reindeer, roe deer, elk, wolverines, lynxes, brown bears and grey wolves.

Trollstigen, Møre og Romsdal
This twisting road was named 'Trolls' Path' in honour of the sadistic creatures who would have enjoyed watching more than 160,000 vehicles each season manage the 11 heart-stopping hairpin bends. The road, which navigates an 850-m (2790-ft) pass beside the Stigfossen waterfall, is open only mid-May to October.

Oslo

Oslo celebrated its millennium in 2000, marking around one thousand years since the first buildings and burials on this fertile land beside the inner Oslofjord. The settlement first became capital of Norway during the reign of Haakon V (1270–1319), who started work on the Akershus Fortress. At this point, the city was known as Ánslo, and later Oslo, probably meaning 'meadow beneath the ridge'. The growing city lost importance during the unions with Denmark and later Sweden. In 1624, after Oslo was yet again destroyed by fire, King Christian IV built a new city, closer to the Akershus, and named it Christiania. The village of Oslo became a suburb outside the gates. It was only in 1925, after incorporating the village with its former name, that Norway's capital was named Oslo.

Many of the city's grandest public buildings date from the period after 1814, when Christiania was made co-official capital of the United Kingdoms of Sweden and Norway. Most of these structures, such as the Royal Palace and National Theatre, are in the Neoclassical style. After Norway gained full independence in 1905, a new generation of Norwegian architects and artists searched for new expressions in order to break with the past. The results can be seen in the Functionalist City Hall as well as Gustav Vigeland's bold sculpture installation in Frogner Park. During the late 20th century and the new millennium, a booming economy, environmental awareness and forward-thinking planners have led to exciting redevelopments of much of Oslo's waterfront, from the shimmering Opera House to the soaring Munch Museum.

OPPOSITE:
Two Boys Running, Vigeland Installation, Frogner Park
In the city's largest park is the world's largest sculpture installation created by a single artist: 212 bronze and granite sculptures by Gustav Vigeland (1869–1943). Vigeland's sculptures, including his hopeful boys reaching to the sky, aim to represent humanity at all ages and in all its complexity.

Barcode Project, Bjørvika
The Bjørvika neighbourhood faces onto the inner Oslofjord. From the turn of the millennium, this former container port has been the focus of dramatic urban redevelopment, with the high-rise Barcode Project at its heart. These multi-purpose buildings were designed with a focus not just on their structures but on the unbuilt spaces between them.

LEFT:

**Krohg Room,
Oslo City Hall, Pipervika**
Oslo's Rådhus is where the Nobel Peace Prize ceremony takes place on 10 December every year. The interior of the building was decorated with murals by celebrated Norwegian 20th-century artists, such as Axel Revold and Alf Rolfsen. The murals in the so-called 'Krohg Room' were painted by Fauve-influenced Per Krohg (1889–1965), depicting *The City and its Environs*. Internationally, Krohg is most famous for his mural in the United Nations Security Council Chamber, located in the United Nations building in New York, which was commissioned as a gift from the people of Norway.

ABOVE:

Oslo City Hall
The Rådhus was begun in 1931 and completed in 1950, after a hiatus for World War II. Designed by Arnstein Arneberg (1882–1961) and Magnus Poulsson (1881–1958) in Functionalist style, the structure is blunt and utilitarian. The facade is clad in oversized bricks, but softened by sculptures and reliefs by Norwegian artists, including nature-inspired Anne Grimdalen (1899–1961).

PREVIOUS PAGES AND LEFT:
Oslo Cathedral, Sentrum
Completed in 1697 but rebuilt in 1848–50 to designs by German architect Alexis de Chateauneuf (1799–1853), the cathedral stands on Stortorvet ('Grand Plaza'). The Baroque interior was restored in the mid-20th century. Stained-glass windows around the altar were created by Emanuel Vigeland (1875–1948), the less-famous but multi-talented brother of the sculptor Gustav.

ALL PHOTOGRAPHS:
Oslo Opera House, Bjørvika
The 2007 Operahuset seems to slide out of the waters of the Oslofjord. Its white granite and marble roof slants to the waterside, creating a sloping plaza. Inside, curving, wavelike walls clad in oak contrast with the soaring window glass and angular columns.

Historical Museum, Sentrum
Part of the University of Oslo's Museum of Cultural History, this imposing building on Frederiks Gate houses Norway's oldest skull, Viking jewellery and weapons, and exhibits on the lives of the indigenous populations of the Arctic and sub-Arctic regions.

BELOW AND OPPOSITE:
Norwegian Museum of Cultural History, Bygdøy
Situated on the Bygdøy Peninsula, this attraction features a large open-air museum where 150 traditional buildings have been relocated from across the country. The 'Old Town' area (pictured left) hosts buildings from old Christiania (Oslo's name between 1624 and 1925) and its suburbs. The 'Countryside' area (pictured right) features wooden farmhouses, barns and mills.

BELOW:
Poached Salmon
Salmon, served poached, smoked or cured in salt, sugar and dill as gravlax, is a staple of the Norwegian diet. Common accompaniments include cream sauces, such as Sandefjordsmør, featuring butter, cream, dill and peppercorns. Vegetables are often locally grown, including asparagus, cabbage and pickled cucumber or onion.

RIGHT:
Delicatessen
This delicatessen sells traditional *potetflatbrød*, or potato flatbread, a product once as central to Norwegian life as stockfish. This dry, flat, unleavened bread could be stored for at least a year, usually longer, making it essential for Viking voyages as well as winter stores. Also on sale are a variety of hot smoked meats.

The National Museum (the National Museum of Art, Architecture and Design), Oslo
The largest museum in the Nordic countries, the National Museum of Art, Architecture and Design houses Norway's public collection of art, architecture, and design objects. The museum's 2022 building at Vestbanehallen in central Oslo consists of the collections of the former National Gallery, the Museum of Contemporary Art, the Norwegian Museum of Decorative Arts and Design, and the Museum of Architecture.

Spikersuppa, Sentrum
In winter, usually between late November and March, the Spikersuppa ('Stone Soup') pond on central Eidsvolls Plass freezes over, becoming an ice rink that is free to all.

BELOW:

The Troll Shop, Karl Johans Gate
In addition to troll merchandise, this souvenir shop sells the famous Marius sweaters, named after the skier, fighter pilot and actor Marius Eriksen (1922–2009). The knitting pattern, modelled by Eriksen, was based on 19th-century Setesdal sweaters. It features bands of pattern across the chest and upper arms.

OPPOSITE:

Karl Johans Gate
Oslo Central Station closes the eastern end of Karl Johans Gate. This cobbled pedestrian section offers shops, cafés and bars. Just westward, toward the Royal Palace, is the Grand Hotel, where each year's winner of the Nobel Peace Prize is accommodated. Playwright Henrik Ibsen is said to have eaten in the restaurant every day in his later years.

Marina, Aker Brygge
On the site of the old Akers Mekaniske Verksted shipyard, this waterfront neighbourhood underwent waves of regeneration after the yard closed in 1982. The works was once the largest shipyard in Norway. Today, the area hosts high-end apartments, shops, restaurants and bars.

RIGHT:
Motherhood, **Vigeland Installation**
Some are amused by this Gustav Vigeland granite sculpture depicting a mother ridden by two children. Others find the work less playful and more disturbing. The figures form part of a central installation at Frogner Park representing the circle of life.

OVERLEAF:
Fountain, **Vigeland Installation**
The first of Vigeland's Frogner Park works to be conceived, the fountain features six male figures straining to hold a vast bowl on their shoulders, intended to represent the burden of life. The work was initially planned to stand outside Norway's Parliament.

***Monolith*, Vigeland Installation**
At the highest point in Frogner Park is Vigeland's *Monolith*, its 121 writhing figures struggling to reach the top of the stone. It took three stonemasons 14 years to transfer Vigeland's designs onto an immense block of granite. The monolith was finally shown to the public in 1944, after Vigeland's death.

BELOW:

Walking Woman, Ekebergparken Sculpture Park, Ekeberg
Opened in 2013, this sculpture park financed by businessman and art collector Christian Ringnes is set in woodland around 2km (1.2 miles) to the southeast of the city centre. It features works by a range of international names, including Salvador Dalí, Lynn Chadwick, Damien Hirst and Aristide Maillol. Sean Henry's (born 1965) *Walking Woman* is both theatrical and oddly naturalistic.

OPPOSITE:

The Couple, Ekebergparken Sculpture Park
The French-American artist Louise Bourgeois (1911–2010) worked alongside the Surrealist and Feminist art movements, but her sculpture cannot be defined by any one style or idea. Seemingly floating, *The Couple* (2003) suggests the transcendence of love, but also a dehumanizing loss of self.

LEFT:
Monument to the South Pole Expedition 1910–12, Fram Museum, Bygdøy
The Fram Museum honours the polar exploration vessel *Fram* and the explorers who sailed on it, including Fridtjof Nansen (1861–1930), Otto Sverdrup (1854–1930) and Roald Amundsen (1872–1928). The last explorer and his team were the first to reach the South Pole, in 1911, and the first verified to reach the North Pole, in 1926. This monument depicts, from left to right: Olav Bjaaland, Oscar Wisting, Roald Amundsen, Sverre Hassel and Helmer Hanssen.

ABOVE:
***Fram*, Fram Museum**
The *Fram* was built for Fridtjof Nansen's 1893 Arctic expedition. To withstand the sea ice, it was given an outer layer of extremely strong and durable greenheart wood and almost no keel to handle shallow waters. It was also equipped with a windmill to power electric arc lights. After later being used by Amundsen for his South Pole expedition, the *Fram* had sailed farther north and south than any other wooden ship.

OVERLEAF:
Gokstad Ship, Viking Ship Museum, Bygdøy
This museum houses three Viking ships found in burial mounds, including the 9th-century Gokstad ship. It is 23.8m (78ft) long and constructed of overlapping oak planks, held together with iron rivets. The ship was powered by 32 oarsmen, plus a square sail on a mast that could be raised and lowered. The ship was unearthed in 1880, along with the skeleton of a tall, broadly built man in his 40s or 50s, presumably an important leader, plus grave goods including three smaller boats, a tent, a sledge and riding equipment.

Viking Ship Museum
The Viking Ship Museum was designed by leading 20th-century Norwegian architect Arnstein Arneberg, who also worked on Oslo City Hall. The building's wings are a perfect framework for the Oseberg, Gokstad and Tune ships. Arneberg was instrumental in creating a new Norwegian architecture that also drew on vernacular traditions.

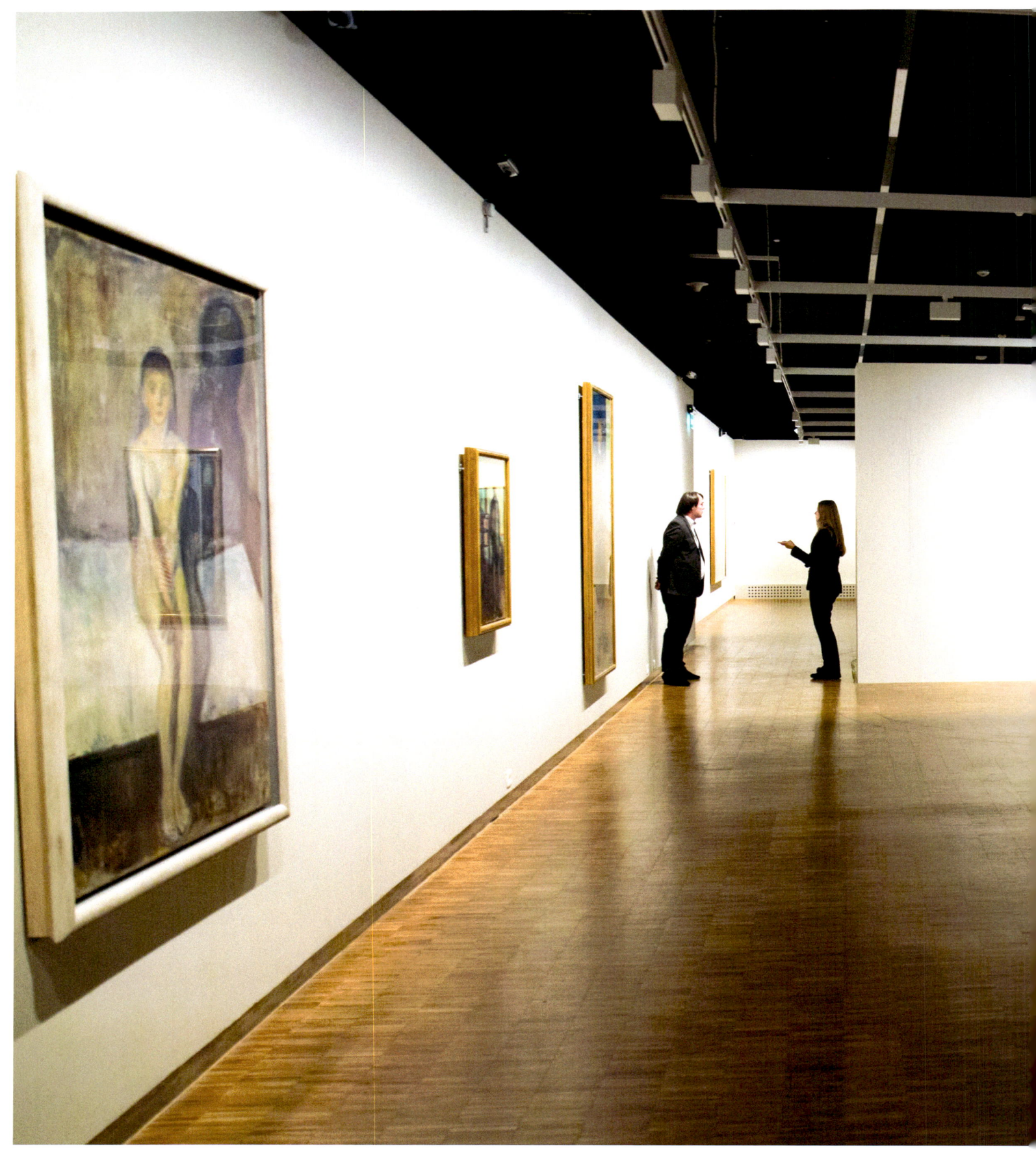

PREVIOUS PAGES AND ABOVE:
Munch Museum, Bjørvika
This museum houses over 1200 paintings, 18,000 prints and six sculptures by the Norwegian Expressionist artist Edvard Munch. The collection moved to a new location in Bjørvika in 2020, in a dramatic building designed by Spanish architect Juan Herreros. Munch's most famous work, *The Scream*, is on display. The museum's version, dating from 1910, was stolen in 2004, but thankfully recovered in 2006. The agonized figure in this iconic composition is arguably one of the most powerful images ever created, able to communicate meaning or emotion to any viewer, adult or child.

BELOW:
The Tiger, Jernbanetorget, Sentrum
The Tiger greets arrivals at Central Station. Created by Elena Engelsen in 2000, the work commemorated the city's 1000-year anniversary. Oslo's nickname is *Tigerstaden* ('The Tiger City'), after an 1870 poem by Bjørnstjerne Bjørnson (1832–1910), who described a meeting between a horse and a tiger, with the horse representing the hardworking countryside and the tiger the dangerous city. Bjørnson also wrote the lyrics to the de facto national anthem.

RIGHT:
National Theatre, Sentrum
The National Theatre opened in 1899 with a season that included Henrik Ibsen's *An Enemy of the People*, about a man who told an unpalatable truth, and Bjørnstjerne Bjørnson's *Sigurd Jorsalfar*, about the medieval king of Norway Sigurd the Crusader. Bjørnson's play featured incidental music by Romantic composer Edvard Grieg (1843–1907). The Historicist building itself was designed by Henrik Bull, who was also responsible for the nearby Historical Museum.

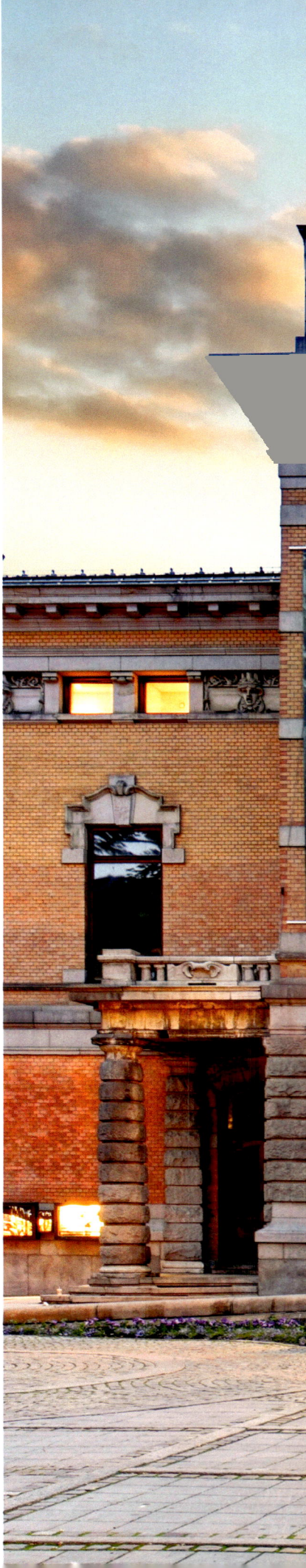

BELOW:
Tekehtopa Café, Meyerløkka
This café restaurant is in the former premises of the Rikshospitalet's pharmacy. The building, on star-shaped St Olav's Plass, was designed in 1872 by Wilhelm von Hanno, an influential German architect who worked extensively in Norway.

OPPOSITE:
Mathallen Oslo, Grünerløkka
Housed in a 1908-built iron foundry, this food hall offers restaurants, cookery courses and shops selling Norwegian and imported specialities. The project was key to the redevelopment of the Vulkan former industrial neighbourhood.

OVERLEAF:
Palace Grill, Vika
With an indoor restaurant, serving only a 10-course menu, and an outdoor backyard with a bar, the Palace Grill has been a popular destination in Vika for decades. For winter nights, there is underfloor heating in the backyard, where DJs as well as local and international bands perform.

Astrup Fearnley Museum of Modern Art, Tjuvholmen
This Renzo Piano-designed gallery is by the Oslofjord, in the rejuvenated docks. Under a curving shell-shaped roof, the steel columns and struts reflect the masts of ships in the nearby harbour. Weathered panels give a more vernacular feel. The building opened to the public in 2012, showcasing international contemporary art including works by Francis Bacon, Gardar Eide Einarsson, Damien Hirst and Cindy Sherman.

Rådhusgata, Kvadraturen
This neighbourhood, just southeast of Sentrum, is named Kvadraturen ('The Quadrature') because of its orthogonal street plan. It was laid down by planners instructed by King Christian IV after the great fire of 1624 destroyed the existing city of Oslo, which was centred on today's Gamlebyen ('Old Town'). The new city, closer to the Akershus Fortress, was named Christiania.

OPPOSITE AND ABOVE:
Grünerløkka
During the 19th century, this neighbourhood northeast of Sentrum became the hub for the city's factories. Today, along with nearby Tøyen, it is central to Oslo's urban art scene, with works by local artists, including Steffen Kverneland and Dolk, and international ones, such as Italy's Alice Pasquini, Spain's Pez and the United Kingdom's Phlegm. The best way to experience the art is just to wander, with Hausmann's Gate as a starting point.

Akershus Fortress, Kvadraturen
Work on the castle began in the 1290s for King Haakon V, after an attack on Oslo by rogue nobleman Alv Erlingsson. The Akershus served as a royal residence until the Kalmar Union with Denmark and Sweden. After 1624, King Christian IV remodelled the castle, adding Italianate flourishes. The fortress has also been a prison, its most famous inmate the escapee and songwriter Gjest Baardsen (1791–1849).

LEFT AND ABOVE:
Damstredet, Gamle Aker
This cobbled street is lined by homes, many of them wooden, dating from the first half of the 19th century. Near the western end of the street is the Cemetery of Our Saviour, where notable graves include Henrik Ibsen, Edvard Munch and Alf Prøysen. The last of these men is best known internationally for his *Mrs Pepperpot* children's books, about an elderly lady who gets into scrapes when she shrinks to the size of a pepperpot.

OPPOSITE:
Akrobaten, Bjørvika
This 2011 glass and steel pedestrian bridge, named 'The Acrobat', crosses the tracks of Central Station, linking Bjørvika and its Barcode Project with the Grønland neighbourhood to the north. This vital connection was a key part of the waterfront rejuvenation project. The bold, asymmetrical structure creates dynamic shadows under both sunlight and its own floodlights.

ABOVE:
Playing in the Air, **Aker Brygge**
Reminiscent of Gustav Vigeland's sturdy nudes on the other side of town, this sculpture by Eli Gabrielsen floats above Bryggegata. Wire netting seems a suitable material for this post-industrial neighbourhood, where cutting-edge design meets renovated warehouses and workshops.

Stortorvet, Sentrum
A market was held in this square, beside the cathedral, until 1889. It was also the site, in 1829, of the Battle of the Square between Norwegian demonstrators and forces of the United Kingdoms of Sweden and Norway. The yellow timber-framed building, dating from 1700, houses the famous Stortorvets Gjæstgiveri restaurant.

ABOVE:

Tram, Stortorvet
The tram network operates in the city centre, while the extensive metro system, known as the T-bane, serves the whole urban area. The first horse-drawn trams went into operation in 1875, while the first electric section opened in 1894.

OPPOSITE:

Oslo Tramway Museum, Majorstuen
This museum in upmarket Majorstuen preserves heritage trams, T-bane trains and trolleybuses. The Oslo trolleybus network, which drew electric power from overhead wires, was closed in 1968. These Høka trams were manufactured in the 1950s.

LEFT:
Sognsvann
Sognsvann Station, just 20 minutes from the city centre on Oslo Metro line 5, is a popular starting point for walking, swimming or cross-country skiing at Sognsvann lake. Cross-country skiing is a national sport in Norway, where some of the world's earliest public skiing competitions were organized by the Norwegian army in the 18th century. The word *ski* itself comes from the Old Norse 'skíð', meaning wooden stick.

BELOW:
Holmenkollen Line, Oslo Metro
The northernmost station in the Oslo Metro, Frognerseteren is a popular destination for summer hiking and winter skiing.
The altitude difference between Frognerseteren, at 469m (1539ft) above sea level, and the lowest station in the network, Stortinget, is 478m (1568ft), the largest height difference within any metro network.

LEFT AND ABOVE:
Holmenkollen Ski Jump
Used during the 1952 Winter Olympics but frequently rebuilt since, this jump is to the north of the city centre. Today, it has a hill size of HS134. Hill size is measured in metres from the top, past the takeoff point, to the hill size point (the lower red line on the photograph above). This point, calculated according to the hill's angle and radius, comes below the critical point (the upper red line), which is the steepest part of the landing slope. When scoring jumps, points are given for metres above or below the critical point. At the time of writing, Holmenkollen's record jump was 144m (472ft).

Sognsvann
Just beyond Oslo's northern outskirts, Sognsvann lake (in the foreground) freezes over in winter, allowing skating and ice fishing. In summer, the swimming and running sections of the Oslo Triathlon are held here. Numerous trails lead deep into the Nordmarka Forest, where blueberries can be picked by the bucketload. Elk, roe deer, wolves and lynx can be glimpsed in remoter areas.

Picture Credits

Alamy: 11 (robertharding), 20 (Simon Kirk), 84/85 (Lars Ostarvik), 96 (Iain Masterton), 98 (Rune Enger), 145 (windgather), 170/171 (Grethe Ulgjell), 198 & 199 (Hemis), 200/201 (Helen Cathcart), 204/205 (Thomas Russ Arnestad), 206 (Jackietraveller Oslo), 218 (Grethe Ulgjell), 219 (Colin Walton)

Dreamstime: 6 (Biletskiy), 7 (Iakov Kalinin), 8 (Ariennewunderkind), 10 (Ryszardos77), 12/13 & 14/15 (Nikolai Sorokin), 18/19 (Mariabk), 21 (Tupungato), 22/23 (Jamen Percy), 24 (Harun), 25 (Kadir Asnaz), 27 top (Santiago Rodriguez Fonoba), 27 bottom (Juergen Schonnop), 30/31 (Tupungato), 34 (Roman Stetsyk), 35 (Sampote Saelee), 38/39 (Davidyoung11111), 41 top (Lillian Tveit), 41 bottom (Alexander Shalamov), 44 & 45 (Michal Masik), 46 (Ondrej Prosicky), 48 (Bikemp), 49 (Marketabenesova), 53 (Niromaks), 54/55 (TasFoto), 56 (Dmitry Rukhlenko), 57 (Dmitry Marhun), 58 top (Tupungato), 59 (Miroslav Liska), 64/65 (Nicola Messana), 66 (Vaitekune), 67 top (TasFoto), 68/69 (Oksana Mitiukhina), 80/81 (Martkal), 104/105 (Polina Bublik), 106 (Serban Enache), 108/109 (Mikolaj64), 115 (Mikhail Markovskiy), 116/117 (Matthew De Lange), 126/127 (Lillian Tveit), 128 (Maximilian W), 134/135 (Anibal Trejo), 136 (Kartouchken), 137 (Paop), 152 (Bojan Mujcin), 154/155 (Morten Normann Almeland), 156 (Mikhail Markovskiy), 157 (Nickolay Stanev), 158/159 (Mikhail Markovskiy), 160/161 (Pablo Hidalgo), 162 (Vichaya Kiatyingangsulee), 178/179 (David Beaulieu), 180/181 (Henrik Stovring), 186 (Saiko3p), 187 (Donland), 190/191 (Saiko3p), 197 (Tomas1111), 207 (Artjafara), 210 & 211 (Arndale), 214/215 (Dmitry Naumov), 217 (Thor Jorgen Udvang), 220 (Bartlomiej Kopczynski), 221 (Marius Wigen Anderesen)

Getty Images: 40 (Wolfgang Kaehler), 222/223 (Morten Falch Sortland)

Shutterstock: 16/17 (Katherine Moore), 26 (Tupungato), 28/29 (mikolajn), 32 (Natalia Schuchardt), 33 (Olga Gavrilova), 36/37 (Morten Normann Almeland), 47 (Giedriius), 50 (ginger_polina_bublik), 52 (Magic Stocks), 58 bottom (Curioso), 60/61 (TasfotoNL), 62/63 (rweisswald), 67 bottom (Bildagentur Zoonar), 70/71 (Toby G), 72/73 (Danita Delmont), 74/75 (bmszealand), 76 & 77 (Jan Miko), 78 (Mr_Karesuando), 79 (Stefano Termanini), 82/83 (Tomasz Wozniak), 86 & 87 (ginger_polina_bublik), 88/89 (LouieLea), 90 (Christian Faludi), 91 (Dmitry Chulov), 92/93 (Ondrej Prosicky), 94/95 (Florida Stock), 97 top (Nicram Sabod), 97 bottom (Grigorev Mikhail), 99 (Alessandro De Maddalena), 100/101 (Boudewijn Sluijk), 103 (ginger_ polina_bublik), 110 (Evikka), 111 (Inspired By Maps), 112/113 (Evikka), 114 (Nacho Such), 118 (Voyagerix), 119 (Red Squirrel), 120/121 (Tatyana VyC), 122 (Nigar Alizada), 123 top (Sergey Kamshylin), 123 bottom (Iakkana Savaksuriyawong), 124/125 (Marius Dobilas), 129 (Homo Cosmicos), 130/131 (Vadim Petrakov), 132/133 (V. Belov), 138/139 (Francesco Bonino), 140 (Tania Zbrodko), 141 (Elvind Kristiansen), 142/143 (peresanz), 144 (Nanisimova), 146 (Pecold), 147 (Drima Film), 148/149 (Spreephoto), 150/151 (Anetlanda), 163 (Felix Lipov), 164/165 (anshar photo), 166 (Yegorovnick), 167 (Byelikova Oksana), 168 (Kollawat Somsri), 169 (Simona Flamigni), 172/173 (Pq189), 174 (Nataly Reinch), 175 (trabantos), 176/177 (Murphy1975), 182/183 (Miroslaw Tarabonowski), 184 (Federico Fioravanti), 185 (Editos Foto), 188/189 (Parry Suwanitch), 192/193 (Morten Normann Almeland), 194/195 (Aleksandra Suzi), 196 (trezordia), 202/203 (Huang Zheng), 208/209 (yegorovnick), 212 (miroslav110), 213 (Kiev.Victor), 216 (futuristman)

Shutterstock Editorial: 42/43 (Splashdown/Sandro Rucci), 102 (John McConnico)